The Mixed-Up Mess

AF584936

Janine Scott

Illustrated by Jon Davis

Emma and Johnny were not happy. Every Saturday, they had to help Mum and Dad clean the house.

"Dusting is boring," said Johnny.
"I don't like vacuuming," sighed Emma.
"But you do like inventing," said Johnny.
"Can you invent something to do our jobs?"

Emma went into the garage.
She crashed and banged.
She hammered and clanged.

Emma had invented a robot!
She put a sucking machine on it.
"This will suck up the dust and dirt,"
she said.

Emma pushed the start button.
The robot made a buzzing sound...
then it got to work.

Up went the dust and dirt,
but something went swoosh!
"Oh no!" cried Johnny.
"Stop!" shouted Emma.

But the robot didn't hear them.
It sucked up everything in the living room.

Up went the rugs.
Up went the cushions.
Up went the books and plants.

Emma ran after the robot,
but it kept going.

The robot went into the kitchen.
Up went the pots and pans.

The robot went into the bathroom.
Up went the towels and soap.

The robot went into the office.
Up went the computer and books.

Emma chased the robot.
"Quick, Emma!" shouted Johnny.
Emma caught the robot.
She pushed the "stop" button.

Whoosh!
Out went the books and computer.
Out went the soap and towels.
Out went the pans and pots.

The robot was happy because everything was neat and tidy.

Emma and Johnny were not happy because...

...all the things went back in the wrong rooms!